FROM THE PARK BENCH

SARA HOLBROOK

RED GIANT BOOKS

Copyright © 2015 Sara Holbrook

From The Park Bench

Red Giant Books
ISBN: 978-0-9905435-1-0

All rights reserved. No part of this book may be reproduced or transmitted in any form or by any means, electronic or mechanical, including photocopying, recording or by information and retrieval systems, without the written permission of the author, except when permitted by law.

10 9 8 7 6 5 4 3 2 1

Printed in the United States of America.

Sara Holbrook is also the author of poetry books for children, teens and adults as well as professional books for teachers. For more information, please visit www.saraholbrook.com

"When we reject the single story, when we realize that there is never a single story about any place, we regain a kind of paradise."

Chimamanda Ngozi Adichie

From the Author:

There is never one side to any story, rarely only two sides. Over the years I have worked in the fields of law, public housing and education. People have told me their stories, kids and seniors, teachers and parents, workers, lawyers, cops, reflecting a myriad of viewpoints. I took notes, lots of notes.

Readers who are familiar with my work may find a familiar line or portion of a poem here and there in this book. Please know, I have not borrowed from my other poems, but rather the other way around – those poems sprouted from this manuscript that has been evolving for over two decades – poetic dialogs, from the park bench.

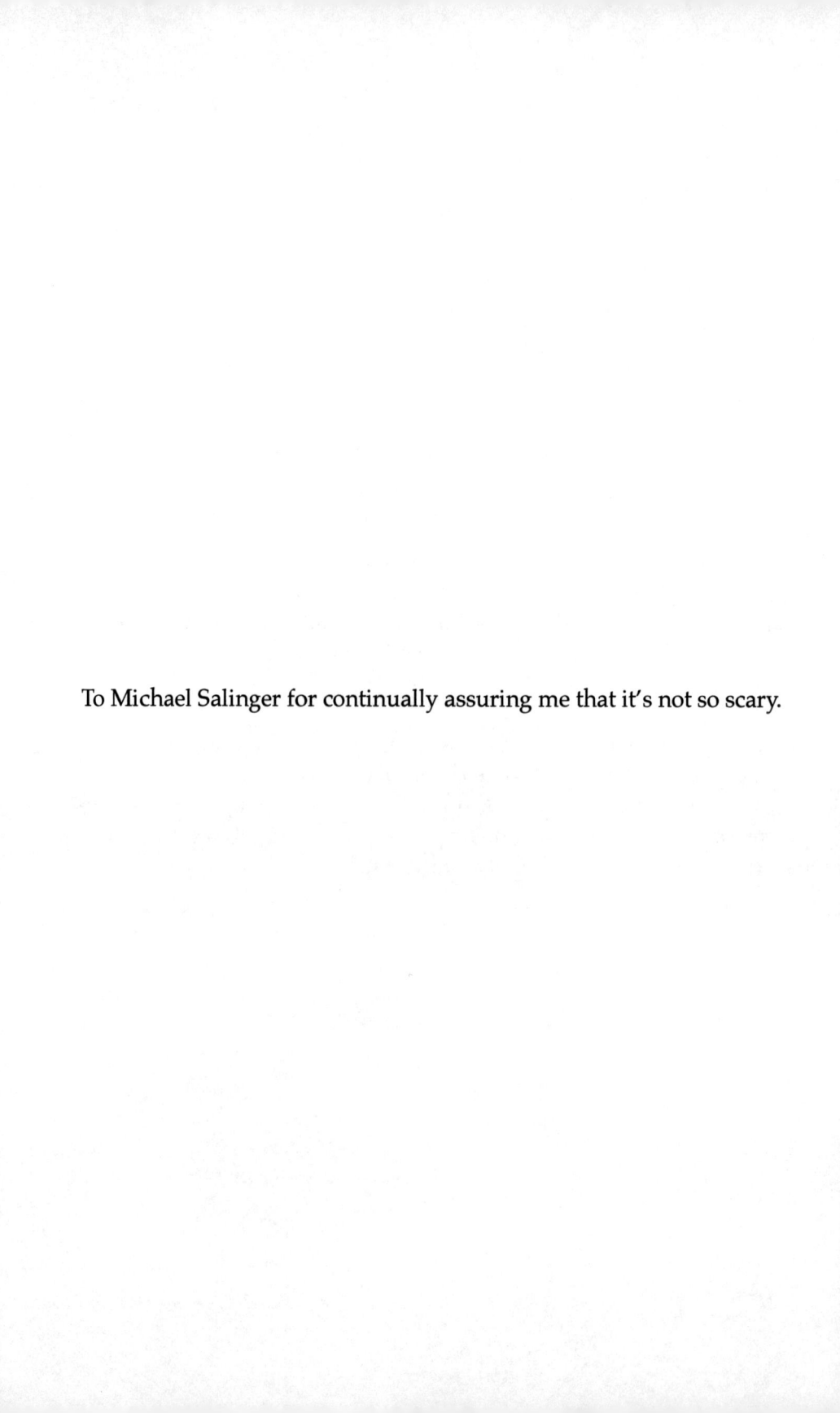

To Michael Salinger for continually assuring me that it's not so scary.

Table of Contents

Politicking 1
Here's the Story 4
Mother Instinct 7
Home 9
Getting Schooled 12
What Man Does 16
Public Assistance 19
Pretty Normal 22
Welfare 24
Enterprising 27
Don't Do It 30
Prejudice 33
Vouchers 37
Booking 42
Somebody 45
Working 47
Nothing New Here 50
Ethics 53
Bologna 56
No Sense 58
Ain't Right 61
Summertime 64
The Environment 67
The Scoreboard 70
Benched 74
Democracy 79
Don't Mention It 82
The Law 85
Just Say No 89
Not Here 93
Privatize 97
Bad Apples 99
Fiscal Management 103
Legalities 106
Lessons 108
Hear It? 111
Poetics 114
Where's It All Going? 117

Politicking _____

Reverend Angus W. Brown
Pastor

Say,
you got politics and you got money in this town.
Rich folks be wantin' a new building, a new street?
It's built next day. They want to shut somethin' down or send somebody down state?
Bam. They gone. Money talks.

Debbie Paulding
Waitress

I got zero time for politics.
Ze-ro. But I'll tell you this,
I'm like tired of seeing people out walking
around on summer days
while I'm hauling ass around this restaurant.
It's like, welfare's a waste and it's flat-out pissing me off.
Whatever happened to only the strong survive?

(Brown)

Poor folks ain't got money, all they got's politics.
Man who shout the loudest, take the hardest fall,
talk to the biggest TV man?
They get by, by gettin' attention where it counts.
Politics is the only way they gonna get what they got comin'.
Even things out.

                                                              (Paulding)

          It's like, I'm tired of paying for everyone else's screw ups.
                                    I feel like, you screw up,
                           you can't set a damned alarm clock
                                    and get your ass to work?
                                                 Fine. Starve.
                               Tell somebody who gives a crap.
                                      Like, it's not my problem.

(Brown)

Somebody always got to be in charge.
It's either the government or the corporations.
One or 'tother.
I don't trust neither one altogether,
but at least with government
I got a vote.
That's politics.

                                                              (Paulding)

                          I just got my paycheck, $2.13 an hour
                                      less the taxes on my tips.
                                       Not that I claim all my tips,
                          but, it's like, well, you get the picture.
                                      So, like, I get my paycheck,
           you know how much it is for two weeks, 71 hours?
                                                        $23.87.
                              To my boss, I'm like, yeah I know.
                         Don't spend it all in one place, right?
       I'm like, something's majorly twisted in this country.
              Federal, State, City, Regional, Social Security.

> My paystub needs like some kinda side-car for deductions.
> So don't talk to me about your damned politics.
> I can't afford the politics we got already.

(Brown)

Without politics and the press, nobody's getting nothing
in this neighborhood.
Somebodies getting lots, mind you.
Always do.
There's lots a money in other people's misery.
But the nobody's?
Nothin'.

(Paulding)

> If I ever wig out and blow someday,
> I'll be like, this paystub is my defense.
> $23.87.
> You think they'll buy that?

Here's the Story _____

Demos Moskowitz

They used to call this neighborhood stacks and spires,
steel mills and churches supportin' immigrant families 'til
their next migration.
Worship the stacks six-day-a-week, the spires one.
Religion industrial style.
Whatever the tithe, no matter.
People, land, water, air -- it all went to serve the iron ore god.
Iron ore capital of the WORLD!
Made in the U.S.A.

> **Jamal Jackson**
> **Public Housing Resident, Age 18**
>
> Top of the list.
> World's most unwanted.
> Young man
> and comin' 19.

(Moskowitz)

Came the Irish Catholics,
who hated the protestants,
who hated the Poles,
who hated the Germans,
who hated the Italians.
The Serbs and the Croats brought their hate with them.
And everyone hated the Jews.

(Jackson)

>Yeah, strong.
>Yeah, smart.
>Yeah high school complete.
>Check male.
>Check no felony.

(Moskowitz)

All that hate waved through the ghettos.
After the war followed the hillbillies, blacks and Latinos
who began to unite the city
in some kind of new-improved hate.
Cultural diversity is a crock.
Everyone wants to be with their own kind
or the closest thing to it
and hate ain't no recent invention.

(Jackson)

>Born USA.
>Check willing to work,
>any shift, anywhere.
>One after two after three
>applications.
>List qualifications,
>young, strong and ready.

(Moskowitz)

So off goes the stack after stack,
no more jobs,
no need for workers whose skills are
strong backs and arms.

Built in obsolescence,
it's the American way.

(Jackson)

Yeah, qualified.
I'm coming,
not obsolete.
People think they know the story,
that they seen and heard my story.
Man thinks he can tell my story by heart.
But, his heart and my heart,
they be coming from different directions.

(Moskowitz)

Them projects there was built for the up-and-outs.
Now it's just for the down-and-no-way outs.
Different warehouse needs these days.
Like them closed up factories,
this neighborhood here just a wore out reminder of what was.

(Jackson)

I got no time for what was.
You can take your what was
on the bus with you.
Buy you a one way ticket.
I'm here livin' in the now;
and my story ain't been written yet.

Mother Instinct

Emma Lou White
Public Housing Resident

Did you hear the one about the welfare mother?
She just having kids and having 'em,
having 'em day after day,
just so's she can get more aid for dependent children?
She don't care none about her kids,
just havin'um for the cash.
Did you hear that one?
The punch line is, she don't exist.
Pretty good one, huh?
Best joke I ever heard.

> **Careen Smith**
> **Age, 15.**
>
> My mama, she told me be careful.
> The boy? He
> told me he loved me.

(White)

What fool gonna have a kid just to get her a pitiful
$152 per month, cash *plus* food stamps? Oh, yeah.
We all'a us gonna grow fat and sassy on that.

> **(Smith)**
>
> The T.V. says practice safe sex.
> The boy? He
> told me he loved me.

(White)

I been mother, I been grandmother.
I seen neighbors, family, lots of folks
come and go, go and come around this place.
I ain't yet to see no mother having babies to get rich or
who done got rich from having babies.
What a down'n dumb joke that is.

                                                        (Smith)
                              My teacher says, don't be a fool,
                                          you stay in
                                                school.
                                       The boy? He
                                    told me he loved
                                                   me.

(White)

Most all mothers gonna want more for
her kids than she got for herself.
That's instinct.
And mother instinct? It don't cost nothin'.
Rich or poor, you's either born with it or you ain't.

                                                    (Smith)
                                                My daddy
                                says, I get pregnant
                                               he's
                                      gonna kick
                                             me out.
                                     The boy? He
                              told me he loved me.

Home

LaTrisha Young
Former Public Housing Resident

Growing up -- I notice.
I'm about eight, all clean, little baby braids.
Decked out! White socks,
dress tied tight, bow in the back.
And I notice.

                                                                Billie Morris
                             Public Housing Resident, Age 11.

            I'm eleven now but I moved a lot when I was a kid.
              Rooming with my cousin and he kept setting fires.
                         We moved five times in one year.
                    We lived at the shelter for nine month,
                      till Mama get this place here.

(Young)

Some of my friends from school,
around their houses, they got grass.
Around my house, no grass.
Just dirt.

                                                                  (Morris)

            This is the first place I ever live, it just have us.
                                  No other family.
                            First day, I just walks in,
                hangs my bag and my coat on the hook.
              Nobody else coat on that hook but mine.

(Young)

So I ask.
"Mama, why we ain't got no grass around our house?"
And she answers.
She says, "We live in public housing, baby."

                                              (Morris)

                              It was real special-like.
              Like when somebody get an award on TV.
                        They hug it and smile.
                Except no audience this time, just me,
                                  quiet like,
                               and that hook.

(Young)

Public?
I'm eight, right?
Public don't mean much to me.
It only mean one thing.
Dirt.

                                              (Morris)

                        I hung up my coat just like this.
                                It was alright.

(Young)

And I'm never so clean again
after that day
'cause I got the shame of that dirt
I got to wear from then on.

(Morris)

Never been any smile bigger than mine,
that day we get our own home.
Not even on T.V.

Getting Schooled

**Moss Peterson,
City School Principal**

More'n ninety percent of the kids in this school
are on free lunches.
Most of the rest, the parents can't even get it
together to fill out the paperwork.
We feed them, too.

**Shaneque Tanner
Public Housing Resident, age 8**

I used to have shoes like that.
Shoes just like yours.
My mama bought 'em for me.
Boys took 'em.
Shoe stealers.
I used to got tennis shoes, too.
Expensive ones, cost a lotta money.
Boys took 'em.

(Peterson)

See that boy?
He was all over me this morning to tell me about his night.
Last night, about the excitement; some guy tried to break in.
His dad stuck a shotgun through the screen door,
knocked out the burglar's teeth.
Six eight-year-olds then held a cabinet meeting

to decide if he should have
blown the guy's head off,
if the blast would have raised him off his feet,
how far the pieces would have scattered.

(Tanner)

They think they so smart.
Last week boys stole my bike.
They so stupid, when they went into the church
for the meal, they left the bike outside.
I stole it back.
I keep the bike inside my house now.
I don't ride outside no more.

(Peterson)

Thinking of my night, last night, I remember.
There were clearly stars, just the hangnail of moon,
the sounds of leaves mixing it up overhead.
I walked the dog.

(Tanner)

I know where you live, I go there all the time.
Everybody in your neighborhood
either a landlord or a doctor.
That's where I'm going to live when I grow up,
except I'm going to be President.

(Peterson)

Kids in my neighborhood fall into their dreams
counting their soccer balls. During storms,
they count seconds between the lightning and the thunder

to help keep the scared away.
Here they count the seconds between the
gun shots and the sirens and the storm
and the scared never goes.

(Tanner)

I can be president.
I can,
'cause my teacher tell me girls just as smart as boys,
and I know it. Boys just stupid bike stealers.

(Peterson)

In my neighborhood bathtubs are where you go to get clean.
In this neighborhood, clean is what you hope for in a mom
and bathtubs are a place to get out of the crossfire.

(Tanner)

You can't be president if you're a bike stealer.
When I'm growed up, I'm going to live where you live
and I can ride a bike wherever I want.

(Peterson)

Mostly, in my neighborhood, if somebody comes to the door
they will ask you to put your donation in a can
instead of helping themselves.
Here you don't even go to the door without your shotgun.

(Tanner)

And I'm going to wear flowered shoes all the time.
Boys don't steal flowered shoes.

(Peterson)

Kids in this neighborhood will tell you, straight up, there ain't no such thing as a free lunch.

What Man Does

Marge Walton
Suburban Homemaker

I was in desperate need of padded, scented hangers
and I saw there was a sale.
Woodhill is the most direct route,
but it does run alongside of the projects.
I always put my purse under the seat,
hit the door locks and don't make eye contact.

Xavier Tynes
Public Housing Resident

We got us a couple of barbecues in the summer.
All the women be cooking like they competing in the
last chance kitchen Olympics.
'Course, I gotta sample it all.
This'ns greens, that'ns.
They dressing, sweet potato pie.
Mmm-humm.

(Walton)

Spring! Blue sky day you just have to get outside
because you hear those shorts and sleeveless shirts
calling your name at the mall.
Me time. Little low fat salad. Manni-pedi.
As I passed the projects,
I noticed people out planting a garden.
Isn't that wonderful?

(Tynes)

I work the city garden plot as best I can.
I got to be feeding it, feeding it all the time.
The soil's just starved.
Soil filled with wild grasses,
greens and wild flowers, milkweed,
it never gets wore out.
Year after year busts out in every direction,
alive, roots all intertwined,
protecting the soil.
Each generation giving life to the next.

(Walton)

Usually I hate to even look at those
concrete block buildings. I mean, who would?
Doors always open in all kinds of weather.
Hallways look so dark and fearful.
Graffiti is the only color you see.
I'm afraid to look, really.
In fact, if anyone's looking back, I don't.

(Tynes)

Man comes along, he separates nature into rows.
Corn here, wheat there, tobacco, beans,
and he plots the soil's demise.
Does his best to kill off the natural
mingling of growth that keeps the soil rich.
Man does.

(Walton)

It just depresses me that people live that way.
In those buildings.
I'd just die.
I mean it, I couldn't live like that.

(Tynes)

                    Some will tell you it works out
                      since we all gonna wind up
                      in the same ground eventually,
                death being democratic like it is.
              Man, plant and beast, side by side.

(Walton)

But that day, people were out planting flowers,
or something. I couldn't tell, really.
But, I thought that was so nice.

(Tynes)

           'Course even dead we put ourselves in boxes,
                              Man does.

Public Assistance

Gus Travis
Public Housing Maintenance Department

My neighbor reads about the housing authority
in the news and
says to me, he's got a great idea.
Light bulbs popping out all over his head.
Says, why don't we take the two-three hundred million
we gonna spend on public housing
next year and maybe the year after,
just give $50,000 to
each family to go buy a house.
Shut down the projects for good.

Millie Trythall
Resident

This here's where I live.
Thirty-eight years I lives here.
My friends, my peoples, my church.
I lives here.
We got everything you got and more.
More neighbors, more love, more danger, more joy.

(Travis)

I say, hey astronaut.
Look around.
What'd you think we're doing?
Driven through the suburbs lately?

(Trythall)

Your neighborhood,
folks goes to church,
mumble they prayers like they ashamed of they own words.
Sings with they mouths closed.
Don't tell me, I seen it.
You gotta walk 100 yards to find you a neighbor
and then, they can't be bothered.

(Travis)

Where you think all that money's going?
Mars?
It's going to pay for public housing windows, furnaces,
cars, computers and doorknobs.
It's going to the contractors and the sub-contractors,
and the sub-sub-contractors,
the minority owned businesses
that ain't no more than a post office box.

(Trythall)

Outside on the wire, hear them birds?
This is they neighborhood too.
They lives here same as me.
Birds ain't afraid 'a the ghetto
and they just little things.
Look it you, big shot.
So scared, you pay big taxes to build
freeways so you can fly over us.
That's what you gotta do, then do it.
But don't be after to move me.

(Travis)

That public housing money's
going to pay for house notes all over this town.
It's going for station wagons,
manicures and lo-cal dog foods.
It's going to fertilize my lawn
which, by the way,
your size 13's are standing all over.

                                              (Trythall)

                                              Me and them birds?
                                              This here's our home.

Pretty Normal

Keri Stallman
Age 17

My mom works at downtown library, so
I got recruited to help with the Christmas party for the kids.
Over at the community college.
First time I'm ever around these kids
or anybody from the hood, you know?

> **Virginia Preslin**
> **Age 17**
>
> You gotta have a sense of humor, you know?
> I was taking the bus over to the welfare,
> got one kid in a stroller, another hanging on,
> waiting at Terminal Tower for a transfer.

(Stallman)

I'm passing out happy meals,
everyone's taking turns,
sort of, you know kids.
They're getting their presents.
The honorable somebody-or-other's playing Santa.
But the real center of attention is the T.V. cameras.
Everyone wants to be on T.V.,
pretty normal.

> **(Preslin)**
>
> I'm just waiting on the bus,
> standing, pretty normal,

like I am here.
Guy comes up,
asks can I spare some change.
Now, look at me.
I look like Ivanka damn Trump or what?
I didn't know whether to laugh or cry.
What's the world coming to?
Can't even take the bus no more,
Next time have to find me a ride.
I mean, what do I look like?

(Stallman)

That's what surprised me the most.
These kids, you hear all these things about them
and there they are
in their little sneakers and jeans and knit caps.
They all looked so normal.
It was fun.
I had a good time.
No, I mean it.

(Preslin)

Seriously?
Sense of humor.
Gotta have it.

Welfare

Ethel Wallison
Former Resident

Brick buildings with steam heat
and windows looked pretty good.
Lots of us lived there and were grateful.
Residents swept the stairs, raked the lawns.
That, along with pride and hope,
was part of the lease agreement.
It was after World War II.
We was vets, DP's,
students and interns from the Clinic.
I never worried -- kids were sick?
I just tapped on a door.
It was all white then, of course.
The projects was our stopping over place.

Tyrone Mosley
Resident, age 12

I'm like, "Ma'am? Ma'am? shh..."
I pick up some cash over there by gas station
if I be quick about it.
"Ma'am'?" I say.
I wash your windshield for a dolla'? I tell her,
don't let the man see.
He be chasin' me off becausa insurance.
She got a million questions.
I tell her, 5th grade.
No, ma'am. Not today. I be watchin' my brother today.

> Oh, we expecting her back. Soon.
> Yeah, well, we run outta milk and the enda the month.
> Maybe I shouldn't mention my little brother, but I do.
> Then I gotta make up an older sister I ain't got
> who I say be watching him when she ain't 'cause
> cause she don't exist.

(Wallison)

We filled them in like water balloons, exploding
all over the city, following the freeways to bungalows
bought with VA loans. FHA.
Government welfare was unheard of back then.

> **(Mosley)**

> "How much this car cost?" I ask her and I guess right.
> Forty thousand.
> Yeah, I tol' you.
> I know cars.
> I let her know I gonna get me a four by four
> soon's I'm old enough.
> But all she want to know is where I live,
> do I need her to call someone and
> how's school.
> "It's boring," I tell her.
> "But I go," I tell her.

(Wallison)

Those estates were beautiful,
hardwood floors and artwork on the exteriors.
Put there by unemployed artists in the depression,
you know.
I can hardly drive through this neighborhood now,

it just makes me want to cry.
Graffiti, stuff hanging out of the windows,
trash all over. Kids out at all hours on school days.
It's all black now,
people milling around with their hands in their pockets.

(Mosley)

She passes me five bucks through the top of her window
'cause she's afraid to roll it all the way down.
But I don't care 'cause, five bucks, you know?
I say thanks and I gotta be goin'.
She make me promise to go to school tomorrow
and I say okay,
because five bucks.
At first I'm pretty pumped over the five bucks,
"fool lady," I'm thinkin'.
I take a break for a trip to the store 'fore I be somebody else
fool.

(Wallison)

Don't those people want a better life?
Good heavens,
what happened?

(Mosley)

Later I'm thinkin',
anybody got such a fine car ain't knockin' herself out
to give up a lousy five bucks to me.
Then I's mad. Five bucks.
What the shit is that?

Enterprising

Olamide Adebayo
Street Vendor

Chai, dem bottom pot boys
no bother me bend down shop.
Dem know I slap and put them for ground,
if de vex me. Na so.

                                  Mary Anne Turner
                                  Office Worker

                                       Ride time's a
                                  daydream let loose
                           by the view from the bus.
          In the morning, having worn thin my mind tape
                          of winning the lotto,
                              Academy award,
                            or Miss America
                       (that tape's 'bout busted),
    I snap in a righteous video and take the front row,
                 window-side daydreaming seat,
  my purse shelved between me and the vibrating wall,
         a canvas bag standing between my calves.

(**Adebayo**)

Dem boys, too many others,
dey NFA.
No future ambition, effa.
Everyday everyday waka waka about,

got nothin' but get enta trouble, what I say.
In this place sell de hats, jewelry, make good chop.
Nobody be take what mine.

(Turner)

That morning bus passes dreams
of me opening my own shop.
Or maybe just a pop up store, selling my jewelry.
My own designs, not cheap imports like
the street vendors setting up on the sidewalks.

(Adebayo)

Watch ya dem.
Call self African.
No African walk with one hand
hold his pants up, pata show on backside samba,
walk like one leg more short dan other.
I am Nigerian before I get America.
Di thing wey my eye see,
me mouth no fit talk am.
Me husband, we two come here
for new life. I give no face dem boys.

(Turner)

But then I see the thugs on the corner and
know I am just the kind of person they would jump.
If I had a gun, I'm the person who'd they'd snatch it from
and give me one right here in the forehead.
And what would I do for benefits?
You think those women street vendors
got workman's comp?
Retirement or 401K?

(**Adebayo**)

Trouble not catch me.
No fear left in my heart.
Life a river flow, you no swim, you sink.
You stand by say, "How now?" you get drown.
Waters got to move, waves de run high.
Area boys be thinking they give me trouble
but it's dem'll suffer most.
Many peoples no savvy how to swim,
but ya, I savvy.

                                            (**Turner**)

                    By the time I reach the office,
              I'm ready to put in my eight hours.
                 On the ride home, I mostly sleep.

Don't Do It _____

Danita Hernandez
Independent Minority Contractor

No way.
You think I'm gonna get hired
by some fancy pants bank to set their tile?
I got but four employees and maybe four dollars in the bank.
Is my company en todo.
We got knowledge, but little money. Sí?

                                           Holly Barnett
                                          Corporate Manager

                                                        I told her,
                                      "They're using you whitey."
                     I told her, "As long and as hard as you've worked
you can't afford to take a job with any housing authority."
                                                    I told her,
                                          "It's career suicide."
                                       Everybody will think:
                A. She must've been drummed out of downtown.
                       B. She wasn't worth much anyway, or
                             C. She's lost all her marbles.

(Hernandez)

My girlfriend told me no do it.
Mama, she say immigration come and send her back
if I take a job with the government.
She and my pop gonna get deported.

She worries like a chicken, peck peck peck all the time.
But I grew up setting tile beside my pop,
taking over when his knees went.
This what I know.

(Barnett)

Let's face it.
People don't make a move like that,
from corporate to public housing,
and recover professionally. I *told* her.
That place just wants to prop her white face
in the window while it's business as usual
behind her back.
I told her, she's bound to get tangled
in something illegal.
Or get her name muck-raked across the metro section.
Those people all stick together, you know.
She will always be on the outside.

(Hernandez)

Everybody say, housing authority, whoa baby.
That too dangerous for a pretty girl like you.
But pretty girls, we got to eat, no?
We must feed our families.
Se dice que, I be broke before Christmas.
I should get job at Walmart and take the food stamps.
They say, *quien mucho abarca, poco aprieta*.
Who wants to grab too much grasps very little.
I say, I don't grab, I don't get nothin'.
Everybody got a story about how my business,
it no work,
and somebody's brother-in-law, he got screwed bad.

Lots more reasons to not do than to do, but I do it anyway.
Practico, sí?

(Barnett)

She wasn't listening, so I called Cynthia
to talk to her and she told her the same thing.
And Cynthia called Jason,
we all told her.
It's impossible for anyone there, but
do-gooders like her from the suburbs
haven't a snowball's chance in a cesspool.

(Hernandez)

Government work.
Housing Authority, I got to go to them.
Minority quotas mean
money upfront to buy supplies.
I paid every other week. I meet my payroll.
Who else gonna do that?
Quién más?

(Barnett)

She's bound to come out smelling like shit.
I told her.

Prejudice

Rufus Dyer
Retired Autoworker

Segregation ain't only a southern recipe, you know.
Come from up north, you bet.
Kentucky? Where I growed up?
You had your whites and you had your nigrahs.
He's either a nigrah man or a white man,
there weren't no meanness 'tached to it.
That's the way it was, I didn't know no different.
We was all wearin' red clay for shoes.

Beavan Brown
Age 7

In history with Mz. Bundy, we be studying
all about how on a day call 911 some terrorists
flew jet airplanes into the twin towers of New York City
Actually, it happened
'cause the guys driving the airplanes
were Arabs and Arabs hate America so bad
they just want to blow us up all the time.

(Dyer)

I don't guess there was more'n 150 living in my village
if you counted all the nigrahs, the whites and the coon dogs.
We was all about trying to keep ourselves segregated
from the hogs and the chickens.

(Brown)

Mostly, actually, I just hate New York.
A'course. 'Cause I hate the Yankees.
Don't you talk about the Yankees 'round my Daddy, ooo-we.
My daddy, my uncles, my whole block.
Man, they don't hate nothin' like they hate the Yankees,
not even LaBron, and they be hatin' on him pretty bad some days, 'for he come back.

(Dyer)

First time I took the train up to Paducah, I was 'bout 14.
I see'd they's a sign by the main station room,
say "color red."
I ask the ticket master,
why you got a room for the color a red?
He say, "No, that there's where the nigrahs supposed to go
to buy their tickets and wait on the train.
'Course they just gonna
buy 'em at this winda same as the whites
'cause I'm only one here,
but the B&O make us mark a room for the coloreds."

(Brown)

I don't think LaBron's so bad, actually as a matter of fact.
He just wanted to be part of a winning team.
He got all the money and talent he needs,
But he wants to be called the champ.
You got to respect a homie want to make it big, even
my daddy admit that.

(Dyer)

First time I ever hear'd the term, "colored" used.
First I seed of segregation.
Far's I could tell, both come from up north same as did the word "hillbilly."
Yankees, pokin' fun at red feet.

(Brown)

But hatin' Yankees, you live in Cleveland,
you just gotta hate the Yankees.
It's cause New Yorkers look down they noses at us here,
Daddy say.
They think they so smart and rich all the time
and when the Yankees win,
it feels like they rub our nose in it.
Even so, my Daddy say when those big buildings got
bombed down,
he and the rest of the guys at the firehouse,
they raise enough money to buy
a new fire truck for New York.
That's a lotta money cause it comes with the hoses
and the siren all included.
The coats cost extra.
That's what my daddy says.

(Dyer)

Them projects over yonder,
most oughta come down after the war,
soon as the houses caught up with the babies.
Now, they just another room marked "coloreds,"
you ask me.

Don't surprise me none projects
was invented up north, neither.
Cleveland 'bout as north as you gonna get 'for you
finds yourself swimmin' on over to Canada.

(Brown)

He say they raise the money, because
even though those people who got dead
and burned up,
some of 'em got crushed up into dust, actually.
Even though all those folks were just Yankees?
They's our Yankees.

Vouchers

Cassandra McDougal
Teacher

Area code 216
where weeds betray neglect across
streets, sidewalks, the hope.
I carried a plastic tub of ideas up the concave stairs and
into that dusty pile of bricks purchased from the local diocese for
pennies on the dollar, leased back
to the national charter school corporation
for ten times market value.
I joined the latest craze: milking profit out of schools
that can't afford books.
Tax payer investment in the futures of millionaires.
Kids?
Can't outsource them, can't put them on the tree lawn.

Brian Pearson
Congressman

All money comes with strings.
Unlike most members of Congress,
I am not a millionaire.
I spend hours every day raising the 9 million or so
I'll need for reelection.

(McDougal)

Door closed on the postered hallway
(whatever those motivational slogans were selling,
kids here weren't buying),
I rearranged the deck chairs.
Success was not in the forecast.
No support staff, no library,
no supplies to dam up the voucher revenue stream.
No unions. No retirement.
Even with the special needs kids counseled out,
this place was poised for disaster.

(Pearson)

Inner city schools are a vortex
sucking kids down a fast track to prison.
Why wouldn't I take money from
companies dedicated to changing the trajectory?

(McDougal)

New math: Experience = liability in education.
Teacher jobs are like cheap T shirts,
shrinking, exposing the belly of the jobs crisis.
Armchair educators decide
there is room for profit in crumbling schools.
Housing prices tanked, but I still have a mortgage.
I took what I could get.
Late September; the first teacher quit.
Some students greeted me with love notes,
some called me white bitch.

(Pearson)

>Upward mobility went out of style
around here along with factory jobs.
And marriage, I might add.
Who's going to give me money for my campaign because
they are dedicated to bringing back marriage?
Even the Little Sisters of the Poor
abandoned this neighborhood and they
got operations in India.

(McDougal)

After five days of trying to call the roll,
after I had thrown myself into brawls,
seven seating plans and been robbed of my wallet,
my identity, my credit, my voice.
After all that I had on account
from a dozen years teaching experience had been stolen,
I gave up. Resigned to my guilt. I quit.

(Pearson)

>This is where I come from.
I can help this area.
But first I have to get elected
and that takes moola.
Stacks of it, millions.
That kind of money ain't coming out of
a neighborhood already has its pockets turned out.

(McDougal)

"If management spent less on campaign contributions
and more on student support services…"

Before I could finish the principal told me
I had crossed the line.
I had to sit through another video on
the benefits of corporate reform
before collecting my paycheck.

(Pearson)

You know who donates to campaigns?\
Rich white guys.\
It's the truth.\
White guys in PACs,\
white guys with their corporate checkbooks,\
white guys with money out of their own pockets.\
All these white guys are not looking for change,\
they like things just the way they are, thank you very much.\
But they are looking to get something back.\
Not evil, just doing business.\
They may not want my constituents living next door,\
but they aren't heartless.\
If they want to make a little extra scratch\
providing educational choices for folks\
in exchange for strengthening my war chest,\
is that so bad?\
Charter schools are a choice is all.

(McDougal)

I drove through tears
back to my own area code, 440.
I swore I would leave all that despair behind.
I pulled the curtains, studied fencing catalogs.
Vows. Promises. More swearing.
No more crossing the line.
No more.

(Pearson)

Prisons. Health care. Housing. Education.
These are businesses
not headed for China or Bangladesh.
The big four.
What we got left.
Privatization means profit.
Profit means political donations.
Don't throw arrows at me.
At least I'm trying to make things better around here.
What are you doing?

(McDougal)

Last night my son brought me a cell phone
he found in the yard. Area code 216.

Booking

Judy McFarland
League of Women Voters

It was one of those luncheons,
the water's warm, the coffee's cold
and the speaker is supposed to put you to sleep.
Then the a representative of the housing authority
stood up to talk.
Such a charming, dignified, woman,
stunning, really.
You have to admire her passion and love for the residents,
especially the kids.
Anyway, seems like the project kids
forget so much over the summer,
she's setting up a summer reading program to help.
They need books.

                                      Otis Freeman
                                   Former Resident

                                    I gave to that book drive.
                                What do you want from me?
                  I don't do that neighborhood any more.
                              I know I grew up there.
                                But that isn't me, now.
          I don't have anything more in common with
                those people than I do with Chinese food.
                    And they both give me a headache.

(McFarland)

Now, there's a project for us, I think.
Couple of phone calls,
pretty soon my garage is a warehouse.
Over 5,000 books and another $12,000 in donations.
The day we passed out the books, it was glorious.
Families swarmed into that rec center.
We even had a table of books for the moms.
Those went, too.

(Freeman)

I climbed aboard the success bus.
Beat the odds.
Started out fighting, like most.
Boxing.
I was too short for basketball and too light for football.
Couldn't punch worth a flip, though.
Took up reading.
Wound up on a token scholarship to private high school
and Yale straight through law school.
No bookie would even give you odds on that one,
so no, I do not want to volunteer.
Are you crazy?
No one down there wants to talk to me.
Don't you see?
I'm too white now.

(McFarland)

I know in the scope of things, it doesn't seem like much.
There's so much those children need.
But I feel pretty good about it.

All those books and we were able
to pay for some rehab on the rec center.

(Freeman)

Go find someone else's tree to climb,
this one's pulled up roots and moved on.

Somebody

Bernard Johnson
Inner City Resident

It ain't what they say, man.
It ain't what you thinkin'.
It's about being the best.
Don't matter you a bus driver,
a bank man or you boostin' cars.
If you doing it, you want it be the best. Right?

Anthony Potts
City Worker

The streets never was kind.
They was more forgiving.
I done time. State time.
Small time, a car's all.
No guns, no money, no carjacking crazies.
Me and a buddy, we go for a ride
lasts two long years.
Thought, man, you can't get away with nothin',
and shackled like a dog in a courtroom
ain't no place I want to be twice.
I done my time and be done.
Second chance.

(Johnson)

If I be drinkin', I want to be the one

downin' the bottle.
Even if I nothin' but a crackhead straight-shooter
then I want to be the fastest straight shooter
there is. Shoot the most.
If I got a gun, then I want it the biggest
cannon in town.
It's like that.

(Potts)

World fresh outta second chances, these days.
Lord have mercy.
Take a drug, take a needle,
take a little sugar from the wrong lady, you gone.
Disrespect the wrong dude?
Go out for a pack of Skittle candy at the wrong time?
Bam.
Ain't no kinda coming back from mistakes today.

(Johnson)

The best is somebody.
Everybody want to be somebody.
Ain't no different than that.

(Potts)

Nobody handing out second chances
for the boys today.
Lord have mercy.

Working

Brenda White
Former Public Housing Resident

Me and Arnold. We do the right thing.
We get out and get us jobs.
Minimum wage, but steady.
Almost full-time.
Not cheaters,
not taking no welfare or social security.

>   **Curtis Parman**
>   **Address Unknown**
>
> I been to the hiring halls, 'cause, well, maybe.
>   Construction companies come in here
> pockets stuffed with millions for urban renovations.
> They got their minority hiring goals and what all,
>   so I think, maybe.

(White)

We wait to tell the housing authority re-examine
that we're working. Wait 'till we're called.
They're supposed to call
once a year, but they usually running
behind. Figure we can push it some
and we need some work reference,
saving up our security deposit to get us a better
apartment and out of the projects.

That's where we're going.
For sure.

> **(Parman)**
>
> Minority? I got that covered.
> 'Course they got that covered too by some
> plumber 1/8 American Indian or whatnot.
> Like most the men around here,
> I'm not officially a public housing tenant
> -- my name ain't on nobody's lease.
> I go on the lease, they lose their apartment
> and their food stamps.
> So I'm not really a tenant, I just live here.

(White)

But my neighbor. She's jealous
my man living with me. Turns us in.
Letter arrives like a nuclear bomb.
Our rent jumps from $80 to $700 per month
and retroactive. 30% of gross pay,
Congressional rule. For a one bedroom
in the projects, ain't the gold coast.

> **(Parman)**
>
> But I go to the hiring halls anyhow on a maybe.
> They gonna hire two or three tenants for this job
> to join the army from the outside
> whose gonna be working here
> over the next two years.
> Maybe they won't be checking the leases that good.

(White)

And us, no food stamp, no health,
no help on the day care.
After tax and rent we can't live.
And the letter say they going to prosecute
for $7,000 back rent.
It'd be pretty good joke if we wasn't so scared.
We skip out the next day.

(Parman)

I got my maybes out all over the place.
I been through three training programs,
got an associate's degree from Tri C,
and I still ain't got me no job.
I was part of Project Hope, Project Care
and project take a seat over there,
maybe we call you in 20-30 years.
Maybe.

Nothing New Here

James Homes
Social Services

Leftover hippies like me
are like leftover mashed potatoes,
you get cold and stiff after a while.
I used to believe in revolution,
like it was coming around the corner, next bus.
Just a matter of time.
Abraham, Martin and John.
All that. I used to believe.

Bordie Price
Inner City Resident

Don't ask me what's new.
Nothin' new here.
This place like what the weatherman call
lake effect,
when the breeze off'n Lake Erie
smell like exhaust.
Air'd be moving, but just churning up old dirt.

(Homes)

It was the Age of Aquarius,
going to find harmony in the universe
and start in my own backyard.
Age makes you far-sighted,
26 years of aging in public housing
means you see nothing but the same

coming over the horizon.
Here, it's 1000 instruments
bleating and cheating,
making chaos
but never a tune.

(Price)

Don't matter how much explainin' I do,
you can't know what it's like to live
in a place where nothing works.
You try and raise kids right 'round here.
Can't even let them out to play.
The whores be doing their dirt in the hall
right outside the door.
Our home.
No use calling the police,
time they get there, if they get there, it's over and me left
answering questions no child ought have words for.
You want to explain an open-mouthed whore
facing an open fly
to a child not tall enough to reach a swing yet?
Do ya?
Do ya?

(Homes)

Every once in a while they change the conductor.
Tap, Tap. We pause and look up.
Conductor changes our chairs.
Switches our instruments.
Singles out some for farewell, solo performances,
lawyers playing back-up,
jingling pocket change like tamborines.

Respectful silence. For a moment.
The conductor gets poised for the downbeat.
But the players, they start where they want,
go where they want,
accustomed to their own ways.
Soon, he's all drowned out.
No one is paying attention.
Pretty soon someone blames the conductor.

(Price)

You got your work place,
your favorite going out place,
your home.
I got but one place.
Until you live without
another place,
you can't know.

(Homes)

Revolution?
That means they wrap another crook in a tux
and drag him in from the wings to direct.
And harmony?
Get you some headphones.

Ethics

Joey DeMarco
General Contractor

You want to know about workin' the projects?
How do you like these apples --
I'm on the job, guy sprints by me,
I realize that ain't a baton in his hand.
Cops running after him screamin', *which way'd he go*,
guns drawn.
I'm talking mother-lovin' shotguns.
It's like Universal Studios.
Real but not real. I don't know if they even caught the guy.
Don't matter. It's all about intimidation down there.

Ron Evans
Housing Authority Architectural Engineer

Twenty-million plus.
It's his job to let out the sub-jobs, to fence it, police it.
To strip it of asbestos, lead and aluminum wires.
His job to put in the windows, new floors,
new roofs, new walls and some grass.
It's my job to watch that he does.
So he does not overlook minor things, firewalls or stairs.
Make cheap substitutions. Shortcuts.

(DeMarco)

The cops try and intimidate.

The young assholes try and intimidate.
The wailin' mothers try to intimidate.
The housing authority intimidates.
And the workers from the outside, we can't just work.
We gotta intimidate too or get caught in the cross fire.

(Evans)

What I've learned here, they don't teach in graduate school,
I can tell you that.
I never learned how to try and bring a building up to code
after firewalls been left out by long gone contractors
and I can put my fist through the walls
from one apartment to the next.
Hell, my textbook only had one code of ethics.

(DeMarco)

I hire off duty Cleveland cops to guard my men. I warn 'em,
"Each one of you swingin' hammers is responsible for
yourself out there."
I lay it on the line,
and I strongly suggest they carry more'n two arms,
if you get my drift.
Yeah, they carry guns, radios.
They never enter a basement or hallway alone.
It's workin' a war zone, workin' a war zone.

(Evans)

What I learned here is that ethics is cultural.
Like, you grow up in the suburbs,
it's okay to cheat on construction work
at the housing authority.
If you grew up in the projects, it's okay

                    to steal from the white contractors
                because they have work and you don't.

(DeMarco)

Maybe we don't have that much trouble,
but you know trouble is always waiting under the table,
a drooling dog waitin' on scraps.
Every afternoon we lock up and get out by 4:00.
Whatever scraps fall on the floor after 4:00,
that belongs to the pushers, the pimps and the whores.
Unspoken agreement.

                                                              (Evans)

                It's okay to skim as long as you call it a "fee."
                            And it's okay to steal
                        as long as you're just doing
                    what you have to do to stay even.
                        The skimmers are everywhere.

(DeMarco)

The intimidation you can never let up on
or the dog'll be right up in your lap.
A snarlin' teeth bared pit bull, I'm talking.
If I pad the estimate or run over,
well that's how it is. Hazard pay.

                                                                (Evans)

                        Some skim off the top.
                        Some skim off the bottom.
                There's lotsa forms a government assistance.
                        You learn as you go here.

Bologna

Frank Novak
Independent Small Contractor

My first mistake was bologna, no joke.
Resident told me one of my painters,
he unplugged her refrigerator and her bologna went bad.
I thought, well probably not, but why argue.
Gave her two bucks out of my pocket.
Good will.

> **Edwina Reed**
> **Resident**
>
> I'm goin' get me a good Jew lawyer, man.
> Painters come,
> I slip in the slime.
> I'm injured.

(Novak)

Next apartment, resident claims
workers drip paint on her $60 pair a shoes.
We negotiate down to $10 on a pair of beat-up shoes
cost no more than $5 new, if they ever were new,
which I doubt.

> **(Reed)**
>
> Look at me. See?
> My back.

> Disabled now.
> No more strength than a ripe banana.

(Novak)

Pretty soon I'm making goodwill donations every unit.
I'm not the Bank of America here,
I'm just a small business.

(Reed)

> Can't work, can't walk, can't do nothin'.
> You owe me, man.
> I'm 'bout ruined.
> See you in court.
> That white, jello-dicked mother tried to kill me.
> You see that?

(Novak)

Learned my lesson.
No bologna stories next time, I tell you.

No Sense

Mijo Stephan
Journeyman Carpenter

Well, that takes the cake.
I'm a carpenter, one of those union workers you read about.
I've been told to slow down.
I've been told to sit down.
I've been told to call in sick.
But this here, I'm telling you.
This takes it.

> **Emerson Grant**
> **Resident, Senior High Rise**

> Ask me how I wound up in public housing.
> I don't mind telling.
> Weren't from taking no welfare money, tell you that first.
> I worked, head man Bond Court Hotel.
> Head man, forty years, workin' almost to 80 them thinking
> I'm just sixty-five.
> I got respect, but no pension. Just the social security.

(Stephan)

The closets.
Too narrow for a hanger, I'm telling him.
Look here, don't have the depth
for a lousy metal coat hanger.
I bring a show-and-tell sample up from the truck.

"What?" he says.
I say, "Look it.
A hanger don't fit in these here closets we building."
"What the specs say," he asks.
Well a'course we followed the specs, I tell him.
"You followed the specs?"
"Sure."
"Then keep buildin' dickhead.
Architectural error ain't our beef."

(Grant)

This here high rise?
It could be nice. Not fancy like some downtown hotel,
but nice, if they'd keep it up.
If you owned a house,
would you let the roof fall into the basement?
Would you board half it up and leave it to the rats and keep
the other half for folks to live in?
This place got no kind of maintenance.
$50,000 a year just to spray for the roaches,
up and down them halls.
I got to empty my cupboards out
once a month for the poison.
But down to the basement -- trash stacked to your eyeballs,
and the trash shoot?
Lord, if that's ever been hosed out once
I'd be damned surprised.

(Stephan)

Like I don't know what he's thinkin'.
He's thinkin' about an inside contract for next winter
correctin' what we coulda made right first off.

I must'a come up lookin' screw-eyed 'cause next you know,
he's in my face so mad his hat's rattling like a pressure cooker
fixin' to blow.
"Don't try to apply logic here, asshole.
This here's owned by the government and logic don't apply,"
he says.

(Grant)

People say we don't take care
of what the government give us.
They don't know.
We just living here, government owns the place.
You know, if I owned a doghouse,
I'd keep it up and 'spect others to do the same.
Don't make no sense not to.

(Stephan)

No sense.
We proceeds to build six high rise floors of them closets.
So I guess he's right, but.
Damn.

Ain't Right

Beronica Clark
Public Housing Resident, age 18

Let's say your daddy die, he leave you a house, right?
And my daddy die, he leave me a house.

> **Tiffany Woods, Age 6**
>
> My mama stole these pants for me at Wal-Mart.
> As soon's she's not looking
> I'm going throw them in the trash.
> They trash.

(Clark)

Say, your daddy owe my daddy when he die.
Then, you owe me the debt your daddy owed my daddy.

> **(Woods)**
>
> At the store,
> I see a pretty little red tutu ballet skirt
> with shiny dots all over.
> It sparkle like a million diamonds.
> I tells my mama
> I want it so bad for my birthday.
> That's all I want.
> That little red tutu.

(Clark)

That debt your daddy owed my daddy
that becomes part of the inheritance,
same as the house.

(Woods)

Only she don't get
me the red tutu ballet skirt.
She gots me these pants.
And then she gots all mad when I opens
up my birthday present and
I throw it on the floor.

(Clark)

Things ain't been right for black folks in this country
since the day we got ripped from the bosom of Africa.

(Woods)

She call me brat.
She say, go to my room and she
gonna knock some sense into me
if I don't be grateful 'cause she gots me a present.
I tell her,
that ain't right.
You didn't get a present for me.
You got one for you.

(Clark)

Don't you act so all that 'round me.
It's easy to be honest when you're rich.

Only, you ain't as rich as you think because you got debts, see?

(Woods)

I wanted that pretty red tutu.

(Clark)

You owe me.

Summertime

Bob Williamson

You gone ahead with your federal programs,
drug preventions and high finance.
Aim your sights at herds of boys,
percentages're all you after.
I go after 'em one at a time.
I take the boys fishin'.

Ramone Melaragno
Age 10

I got recess detention all this week at school.
I don't care.
You think I do?
No way.
They don't make me.
Don't matter.
Not fair.

(Williamson)

I don't write no grants. Don't got time for meetings.
I don't talk to no suits.
I take the boys fishin'.

Maxine Walsh
Housing Estate Activities Director

I'm already dreading summer.

> We've got to get some programs in here for the kids.

(Williamson)

See that raggedy station wagon?
Stays on the road by the grace of God Almighty.
I pick them up where's they's hanging out
pickin' up nothin' but bad habits.

> **(Melaragno)**
>
> Not my fault, he smacked me first.
> I'm gonna kill him.
> I don't care.
> Get me some bullets and chrome.
> Blow his face right off.

>> **(Walsh)**
>>
>> Secretary of HUD was through here
>> for a photo op a couple summers back.
>> He flipped a basketball into this milk crate
>> nailed to the wall and made a personal promise to the boys
>> to get them a real hoop.

(Williamson)

I give 'em bait, a rod, a hamburger here,
a Coca Cola there, and a bandaid when they need it.
I'm a low budget operation.

>> **(Walsh)**
>>
>> Well, the milk carton's still there,
>> basketball court went to someone else's ward,

boys are still throwing themselves up against a brick wall.

(Melaragno)

I'm gonna ditch school for good,
run away from school,
run out these projects.
So far, far, far, far teacher can't see me.
Principal can't see me.
Nobody see me, not no one, no more.

(Williamson)

Folks got too many reports to write.
My kind of economics is one on one.
I grab 'em. I hug 'em.
And I take 'em fishin'.
One at a time.

(Walsh)

Come summer, that drunk'll be back
picking up kids to go fishing in that death trap he calls a car.
If I could land one grant for
books, a real basketball court.
It wouldn't take that much,
two million and two years.
What do you say.
Let's try to get something on paper
by March.

The Environment

                                              Edna Porter
                                       Inner City Resident

                                                     Racial?
                                           What else you call it?
                                     Meetings. Schmeetings. Shit.
                                    We fixin' to march on they ass.
James McIntyre, CEO

I'm the one they're after.
My business is over the hill,
in the flats by the river, come see.
Come by cab.
This neighborhood's hell on cars,
if you don't get ripped off, the ash'll pit your paint.
Depending.
                                                    (Porter)

                                              Look here at this.
                                                 Newspaper say
                           the lead content in the air 'round this place
                                       is 2,000 time the legal limit.
                                   Ain't but black folks living here.
(McIntyre)

Well, depending what's cookin' that day in Hell's kitchen.
Yeah, the Nader-raiders shut me down once or twice a year.
I scream. They scream.
Makes good T.V.
Pretty soon I'm back in business.

(Porter)

You think we able to drive 2,000 time the legal limit?
Can we drink 2,000 time the legal limit?
Can we run up our charge up 2,000 time the legal limit?
No sir.
But the white man's business
in black folks backyard 'loud to.
Am I right?

(McIntyre)

You want to talk environment?
Right. Yeah, this environment is dangerous.
Life threatening, but that ain't my fault.
This here's the hood.
Hell, it ain't safe here any time a day.
I carry a gun and look both ways just crossing the parking lot at noon.
Pollution is the least, right?
I didn't create this environment.

(Porter)

I can tell my babies don't eat the paint.
Tell 'em, don't play with knives.
Tell 'em, don't mess with drugs.
But you tell me how I'm gon' to keep 'em
from breathin' the air.
A body got a right to live, dammit.

(McIntyre)

City should thank me crawling on their knees, I'm here.
Paying taxes, not cheap, to operate where you gotta realize,
Citibank ain't about to open no office.

                                                            (Porter)

                    Come summer, we closin' them down for good.

(McIntyre)

C'mon, things're better.
I mean it's still healthier to commute by tank,
don't get me wrong.
But, hell, the river ain't caught fire in years.

                                                            (Porter)

                                        You think anyone'd put up
                                        with this in white folk's home?
                                                    The suburbs?

(McIntyre)

That's progress, no?

                                                            (Porter)

                                                            Hell no.

(McIntyre)
                                                            (Porter)
Am I right?
                                                            Am I right?

The Scoreboard

If we lose,
That's okay.
You will work
for us someday.

Joshua Sayles,
Social Studies Teacher, Part-time Roofer,
and Inner City Football Coach

I got on the bus thinking
this game's bound to be a bloodbath.
Suburban team's been practicing
for over a month.
They got line coaches, assistant coaches,
assistants to the assistants and a lighted field.

Hank Hadden
Suburban Football Coach

It's just customary.
A custom developed over the years.
We want our boys to feel confident
heading into the season.
So's the pre-season game tradition
is that we win. Plain and simple.
We choose an opponent certain to
give us a good solid win
heading into fall, see?

(Sayles)

Me and my assistant coach,
we were packing up the gear,
we have exactly 20 helmets.
That means defense and offense
going to be sharing.
But I tell the boys not to worry,
we got 'em covered.
I tell 'em they're strong. I tell 'em they got heart.
They even have new uniforms.
Got a real sweet deal
from somebody's uncle with connections.
Fundraisers, a little grant money.

(Hadden)

Don't start with me. Do not start.
I am tired of living in the shadow of
a racial scoreboard where
white faces are public enemy #1. The entitled.
Inner city team. Poor poor underdog.
Everybody wants to root for the underdog.
Kneejerk liberal reaction.
Is that what you mean by racism?

(Sayles)

So, we have four days to workout
before the game.
That's all the district'll pay for.
Opening the locker rooms,
paying the coaches.
That all takes money.
I mowed the practice field my own damned self.

(Hadden)

Racism. The word smells bad, and like the kids say,
IKES! them who smelt it dealt it.
Start talking racism, that makes you the racist.
I know our team is all white
and East Cleveland's is black.
I look blind?
But race? That's not even on the table these days.
For certain race is no longer an issue in football.
Why, most of the best pros are black.
If you'd take time to examine the situation
you'd see that we're the damned underdogs.
Christ, their boys are 18-20-years-old, scary as hell.
Who knows if most of them are even enrolled.
I have my doubts, let me tell you.

                                              (Sayles)

              I didn't tell the boys, a 'course,
    but I never went there thinking we were going to win.
            Get out there and play your best game, I told 'em.
                                    And then the rain.
              Lord almighty. The clouds just let loose.

(Hadden)

Man, it just poured.
That was probably it.
Rain waving in sheets in the lights.
Lines washing off the field.
No lightening though, so no one called the game.
Looking back, maybe,
I don't know, maybe
I shoulda said something.

But if I'd called it, they would have
gotten credit for the win.
See? And we needed the win.

(Sayles)

We were down six when the rain started
and it just put out the fire in that other team.
We scored immediately.
Thomson kicked the extra point.
Miller was the ball carrier. Up one.

(Hadden)

Shit, their uniforms were so cheap
they bled all over the field.
We didn't get beat by the red and white Spartans,
we got beat by the pink fairies.

(Sayles)

My boys played through it all, the rain,
the ruined uniforms,
the mud.
They were men out there.
I couldn't have been more proud.
No amount of rain could
dampen their spirits.
Until we were loading back up on the bus
and we heard that chant.

If we lose,
That's okay.
You will work
for us someday.

Benched

Phil Macey
Age 18

I live here, ya know.
No, I mean right here.
I aged out of a bed in a room
with a roof and a bathroom.
Lately I got this bench. Whatever.

                                      Jonathan Chambers
                                      Head City Librarian

                                              I've read Balzac.

(Macey)

First 8 years I was in foster,
I'd dream of my mom coming back
to get me. I'd hold my pillow
like she was gonna hold me.

                                                  (Chambers)

                                                In French.

(Macey)

I ain't crazy, in case you'z wondering.
And I wasn't abused
except for the nine times
they put me on the freakin' news

on *A Child is Waiting*
and got the crap kicked outta my heart.
I look familiar, right?

             (Chambers)

              And Hegel.
              In German.
     I can recite King Richard's soliloquy
       and the Pulitzer Prize winners
        in poetry for the last 30 years.
Two master's degrees from the University of Chicago.
      I keep journals of the books I have read.
           I'm on volume 10.

(Macey)

The thing about foster
is you got nobody.
Miz Jackson wasn't bad,
but when I got to be eighteen,
she had to put me out cause
the state stopped paying.
She's got four beds and that's her job.
I get that.
But where do you go? All grown up, no place to go?

             (Chambers)

           It wasn't sudden,
          like an earthquake.
         More like a slow leak,
      but the love of literature drained
        from this neighborhood.

(Macey)

She helped get me into a motel, week to week.
And then she left, so it was pretty easy for me to go rogue.
Think about it. I got nothin'.
No bicycle, no pictures of me growing up.
Got my coat took off me waiting
for the school bus last spring,
had my toothbrush in the pocket, dang it,
so I'm traveling light for now.

(Chambers)

I am a living memory.
The smell of varnished wood,
the crack of a new book,
the stamp stamp of due dates.
Quiet sounds, books sliding from shelves.
People browsing in the aisles,
sun crackling through the stained glass windows
coloring rainbows on the floor.
This morning I cleaned up
feces from the floor.
On my hands and knees.
In what's left of the 800 section.

(Macey)

I tried offing myself, more'n once.
I was fourteen, sixteen, I forget.
But it seemed so pathetic
'cause my funeral would be like --
crickets. Nobody there.
Don't nobody care about kids like me,
not even God.

               (Chambers)

               We hardly ever loan a book.
        I keep soap and toothpaste in my desk for lending.
           Many of our constituents are schizophrenic,
                            addicts, runaways.
                 I would catalog most as homeless,
                  but they don't have call numbers,
                the world doesn't even know they exist.
              Ours is the only public restroom around.

(Macey)

Especially God. I am off his radar.
Totally free.
How many people can say that?
Not much is free as me.
I don't even have dreams any more.

               (Chambers)

                            Books?
                    Oh, most are retired.
             We have 35 computer stations now.
            People cruise the internet for videos
                  cats playing the piano, porn.
    Some fall asleep on the keyboards until their time is up.

(Macey)

Come winter? Who knows.
Man, that's months from now.
I got today to worry about.

(Chambers)

There's no use for me here,
this place needs a social worker.
No one needs an intimate knowledge of the Romantics
to say, time's up, station 10.

(Macey)

You got any extra cash?
Change?

Democracy

Jane Drew
Public Housing Intake Worker

A large woman thumps past. Thumps.
Thumps past my office.
Thumps. Thumps, toward the ladies room.
Sounds of water running,
a squeaky door slaps against the wall
and oozes to a bumpy close. Thump. Thump.
I look up as she passes again.
Dark hallway. Dark clothing. Dark hands.
White toilet paper. I watch after her passing.
She stole the toilet paper.
Also government issue, 2 rolls per day.
Issued by the same government that will murder a mountain
of forest for the paper
it takes to purchase a pencil through proper procurement
procedures,
will issue food stamps for popsicles, kool-aid and tater tots,
but not for toilet paper like it's some privilege that poor folks
don't need.

> **Olah Johnstone**
> **Prospective Tenant**
>
> Comeuppance waitin' on you.
> It waitin',
> crooked as you are.
> It waitin'

>   like a cat switchin' its tail,
>   going to crack you, soda cracker.
>   It knows how you take peoples'
> money to checker jump names on your waiting list.

(Drew)

I rub at the crow's feet are deepening into my mother's face
and listen to her leaving.
She stole the toilet paper.
The clock silently mouths that it's just 3:05.
I wait for a moment,
reluctant to go once more against the mountain,
knowing the thin air makes me lightheaded. Finally I move.
"Ma'am, did you take our toilet paper?"
She looks straight ahead,
two rolls propped on knees flung wide.

(Johnstone)

>   Comeuppance
>   going to tap its fat foot
>   while you pay back
>   the dignity you stole from me,
>   waiting.
>   Waiting in this hot room
>   smell like it ain't changed its diapers.

(Drew)

She is slow to acknowledge my presence, then in a glance
reminds me I am too tall, too well-dressed, and too
goddamned white.
"I need it," she replies.
And that need, I know is not entirely selfish.

That need embraces the needs of her children, her
grandchildren, maybe a neighbor.
But not the neighbors
with whom she shares this waiting room.
"I have to ask for it back,"
I say, citing the needs of the others.
Reluctant herself, she complies.

                        (Johnstone)

            Oh, if they is a Lord above,
            comeuppance going to get you
            for taking your lunch break,
            me and four babies hungry.
            For talking so mighty.
       For not even using those fancy fingernails
            to flip a few files
before you say ain't nothing for me again.
I waited today like I waited two years on your list.

(Drew)

Practically speaking, she is a republican.
I retreat to return the basics to the necessary place,
dizzy with democracy.

                        (Johnstone)

      But comeuppance be waiting on you, bitch.
                Then, crack.
      White ain't nothin' but the color of my spit.

Don't Mention It

Miriam Feinstein
Resident, Senior High Rise

I come across down below, same as you.
I lost brother, sister,
fevers, murder hunger, same.
We were slaves on the other side.
Here, we were scraps in the sweatshops,
little scraps, we were.
Tiny little scraps.
I work before I remember.

Thomas Bryant
Auditor

My office mate,
she came in with the newspaper under her arm.
Says, the press really gave us a
Rodney King beating this morning.

(Feinstein)

I know the look of hate,
I felt its stick on my back,
the flames of hate burning my feet.
I run, like you.
I run. I fight.

                                                        (Bryant)

            Maybe, it's Friday. Or maybe I have too much coffee,
                                            but I let loose on her.
            I tell her, don't you ever talk to *me* about Rodney King.
                                   Not till the cops answer *your* 911
                                       calls with their middle fingers,
                             not till they drive through the stop signs
                                              in *your* neighborhood,
                  and make a living shooting after *your* friends.

(Feinstein)

All the way, I carry the pain right here.
Pain for those who make it,
Pain for those who don't.
That is my pain.
My pain.
My pain hurts.
Same.

                                                        (Bryant)

                Don't talk to me until you get slammed up against
                      a fence, the cold metal cutting into *your* face,
       slippery with sweat and anger, *your* school books scattered,
                       papers all over in the wind and *you* pinned,
                  and told to spread 'em and all *you* doing is coming
                           home to the projects from Cleveland State.
                              Don't *you* talk to *me* about that.
                                                             Ever.

(Feinstein)

So, enough already.
Give me some peace, a needle.
Here, we make potholders,
afghans.
We make, we sell.
It's a life.

                              (Bryant)

            She says it's just an expression.
I tell her she hasn't earned the right to use that expression.
            I sit down mad and she sits down quiet.
            I know she didn't mean any harm, but
            it shows her lack of sensitivity to what it
                        means to be African American.
            Ignorant and racist, I'm thinking.
            Neither one of us says another word all day.

(Feinstein)

Enough with the talk.
No more fight.
Enough.

The Law

Mike McCann
Housing Authority Police Officer

Here, let me shut the door.
You want to know what I do with
this badge and my gun? Let me tell ya.
I bust niggers.
You shocked? Go 'head
with your pansy-assed white guilt.

> **Charles Prince**
> **Urban Resident**
>
> We both be the man on the street,
> but we from different streets.
> See?
> My grandmother always be tellin' me
> I got to get my ready ready.
> I got to obey the law, got to go to school.
> I got to work my ass off
> at some job like a field slave
> so's I can graduate from these here projects
> to that senior high rise over there when I old.

(McCann)

You scared a that word? Nigger?
I'm not. I'm front line, you hide behind me.
I tell you what makes me shit in my britches scared.

Guns scare me.
Nigger boys with guns in particular.
Most of 'em ain't got the sense god gave gravel
and they carrying guns.

(Prince)

See, I know what I'm needin' now,
I don't know what I'll be needin' later.
Maybe I be to old to appreciate it, see?
Or maybe I be dead.
Ain't no job serving or shoveling going to get my ready
ready, anyhow.
You hear what I'm talkin' about?

(McCann)

My whole family's cops.
My dad, thirty and out, 2 uncles, my brother.
I'm kind of the black sheep cause
I work housing authority force for the past years.
Still working to get a spot on the Cleveland
force or some cush suburb where enforcing the law
means breaking up teenaged parties - my salary
would double overnight.

(Prince)

The laws, see, they was made to protect the rich.
Take the law say I can't steal your car.
Well, you gotta admit, that law kinda slanted in your favor
'cause you the one ownin' the car. See what I mean?
See, I need a car in the winter
for me and my family same as you.
The law's there to protect you and your family from the cold.

>   Don't protect mine. Right?
> Law say my family wait in the cold at the damn bus stop,
>   till our face froze and cracked, not yours.
> You and your government, the "white house," you got it?
>   You make laws to protect *you* and then you want *me* to
>   obey them laws.

(McCann)

Meantime, I answer calls by
inching up pissy hallways at 2:00 in the morning
for $11 a hour. Usually 'cause some
nigger beating up on some other nigger.

>   **(Prince)**

>   On my street, we got our own law.
>   Go like this -- see a fool, use a fool.
> You come around here, dollar bills hanging out all over you,
>   somebody gon'take it, chump.
>   And then you be yellin',
>   "Time out."
>   "Not fair."

(McCann)

It's stupid, I say.
Man, let 'em if that's what they want to do so
goddamn bad.
Sometimes I'm busting the nigger and
sometimes I'm just not available.
You know what I mean?

(Prince)

Well, the world ain't a fair place, that's a fact.
Ain't that what your law be telling me and my kid freezing
our ass off at the bus stop?
The world ain't a fair place,
and we supposed to get used to it?
Yeah, well, you can get used to it easy as us.
So, get used to it.
Chump.

Just Say No

Paul Mason
Cleveland Police Department

Talk about a waste of public funds.
Next time, let's just have a bonfire,
bags of money and a match.
I'll bring the marshmallows.

> **Rick Niper**
> **DEA Department of Justice**
>
> First, I laid out the game plan for my guys.
> Task force guerrillas going to pull out whoever's
> in the crack house unit.
> We're there to wear our letters.
> DEA.
> We were there to be seen.

(Mason)

I counted a dozen Housing Authority blues,
eight CPD black and whites,
the heavy metal van,
a dozen guys in flack jackets,
at least 20 undercover dicks,
the task force maniacs,
the DEA office,
six workmen armed with staple guns and plywood
for the board up,
housing authority and health department brass

at a bazillion bucks an hour
and enough fire power to take out Kabul.
Shit.

LouEtta Mars
Resident

Where's my baby?
You seen my baby?

Rick Niper
DEA Department of Justice

Had my men in full SWAT gear,
that's the important thing.
Vests and helmets.
Wait 'til the T.V. cameras are rolling,
then you face 'em head on.
I want the public to see every one of those three-inch
DEA letters.

(Mason)

You know what this bust got us?
Two sorry-looking guys long lost the
coordination to keep their pants up,
bare-assed, barefoot, on their knees up against the fence
and some zoned-out hillbilly chick fallin'
out of her tank top screamin',
"Where's my baby?"

(Mars)

You can't arrest me, man.
I gotta...my baby.
I ain't got nothin',

no crack,
no nothin'.
Damn you.

**Rick Niper
DEA Department of Justice**

Me? I came armed with a press release.
All comments to be handled by me.
Everybody with a cell phone
thinks he's a reporter these days.
Nobody else gonna say word one.
I don't want them going viral talking like thugs.
Their job was to get the letters in the picture.
No bullshit, this is about public confidence
and credibility.

(Mars)

I want my baby.
Where the hell's my baby?

(Mason)

I don't know sweetheart, where'd you leave it?
Her, we can't arrest.
So that's it. Two pitiful losers in jail,
and the public trough lightered about 12-15 g's.

(Mars)

Get outta my face, you asshole.
You ain't got no place for a baby.
Does ya?
Does ya?

Rick Niper
DEA Department of Justice

No reason for my guys to go inside the building,
let the police do the dirty work.
Still I warned 'em to turn their cuffs down
or they'd be collecting more bugs
then they know what to do with.
Hold their weapons to the side, like this.
Don't cover up the letters.
Show the flag.

(Mason)

See those two guys having a smoke across
the street, the two with the vinyl briefcases?
They're the one's been doin' business on this block.
This circus is just an intermission for them.

(Mars)

You go bust s'body else's ass.
I got my baby.
You got nothin'.
Where's my baby?

(Mason)

I love this job.
No shit.

Not Here

Marilyn Farmer
City Councilwoman

I'm angry, that's what.
Look at all this.
This is not supposed to be happening.
Cameras, the board up.
I was in the meetings to plan this.
It is not supposed to be happening like this.
Not here.

                                            Herb Jones
                              Housing Authority Police

                Crack alley, that's this stretch here,
                          but that's the least of it.
                  You got your meth, your molly,
cocaine, straight heroin and hillbilly heroin. Oxycodone.
                Inner city's some kind of free trade zone
                              for crime and drugs.
            'Course folks also think illegal drugs'r
                          some kind of a black,
                                inner city disease.

(Farmer)

Illegal drug use?
I'm positively militant on the subject.
Drugs have changed everything around here.
Only thing I know of makes a person lose
interest in everything, even a mother for her babies.

(Jones)

But, listen to this one.
Last spring we set up a sting with the task force boys and
city boys, right here.
Video, hidden mikes, the works.
Easy as hauling walleye outta the lake.
Bait, snag, pull.
Bait, snag, pull.
Bam, bam, bam. 72 in one night.

(Farmer)

We got to take a stand against the pusher.
We got to take the streets back for families.
We got to stop the selling of drugs
to our mothers and babies.

(Jones)

Couple a our guys selling, couple a guys cuffing.
Couple transporting downtown
and we get to keep buyer's cars.
That's right, we split 'em up there on the spot.
Housing Authority cops net a red Jeep, a Corvette and a
brand new Charger.
Dress 'em out with emblems and patrol in them,
makes a statement.
What a haul, 50 some cars and 72 collars.

(Farmer)

A public bust -- it's always a good thing.
Toilets flushing all over this block
and that one and the next.
Makes the whole city a little nervous, and I do mean

everybody.
You think folks outside of this neighborhood
aren't benefiting from the drugs?
Think again.
This is a plague on all our houses.

(Jones)

News boys gonna love this one, right?
Hand deliver the release, the names and addresses of the perps to the papers.
Next morning there's a real nice write-up on the sting,
but no mention of the fact that 68 of those arrested are white with suburban addresses. No mention on the T.V.,
nothing on the radio.

(Farmer)

People taking drug money all over town,
taking it to the bank.
The car dealers taking cash for cars, the malls, the jewelers.
You name it.
Any bust is a good thing.

(Jones)

Me to the reporter -- "Hey, Joe, what gives?"
He sputters,
"You know I can't write that the perps were white
any more than I could've identified them as black."
Oh, yeah?
Well, if they'd been black, believe me.
You'd've found a way.

(Farmer)

But it was supposed to be happening in my ward.
That's all I'm saying.
I helped plan it and
the first one's going to get the most press.
And it was supposed to be my ward, dammit.

(Jones)

Keep the disease confined to the ghetto,
maintain the healthy image around the perimeter.
Nobody wants to face facts.
Poverty and crime, they're contagious, man.
Nobody's immune.

Privatize

Matt Lenz
Section 8 Housing Inspector

Privatize public housing.
Privatize the schools.
Bankers, lawyers,
the pinstriped rich cry, "Privatize."
So they can pay less and make more.

Yvonne Taylor
Section 8 Resident

I don't have that much but,
thank you Jesus, we doing okay.
You're welcome anytime.
Most of my furniture come from the church donation.
We're nothing fancy.
But I have to be cleaning all the time.
Cockroaches like lightning to a rod with crumbs.

(Lenz)

I say, privatize? Yes!
My clipboard holds forms to check.
I inspect private Section 8 homes.
Fire alarms. Hand rails.
I count outlets,
insure that housing quality standards are met.
Privatize, yes.

Too much money to repair public housing.
Too many employees
with tax dollar paid salaries and benefits.

(Taylor)

This apartment building's bad as ever.
It's stuffy, you know, the windows are fixed
so they can't open but one inch
and the air conditioning's been out all summer.
No, I don't complain.
I pray, a lot. Jesus brung us this far,
he gonna deliver us from this too.

(Lenz)

Taxpayers, you only pay twenty-two-thou a year for me
to inspect apartments in my BMW.
My benefits are paid by private enterprise.
Privatize?
Praise the Lord.

(Taylor)

Landlord said when I moved in,
first complaint and he'd send me back to the projects.
Here in the Heights, the boys are in school
and they doing real good.
Haven't had to hit the floor once.
Last school they in, four kids got shot first semester.
We're here and that's the most important thing.
The rest, I say,
this too shall pass.
Praise the Lord.

(Lenz)

Yes.

Bad Apples

Mio Mostrianni
Grocery store owner

This grocery been in my family 65 years.
I'm closin' up
'fore some meth-head uzzi me into swiss cheese.
My regulars gonna have to take the bus to
buy apples or a tomato
or go to that rug peddler down the street.
Bandits, all of them Arabs.

               Sferra Sirallyi
       American Civil Liberties Union

               First of all, I am not an Arab.
                      And I am not white.
                           I am Persian.
                 Second, I resent being treated
               like I have a bomb in my pocket.
                This country's has been on fire
             for the entire length of its short history.
Black, white, rich, poor, from every country in the world.
                         A volatile mix, no?
                 America is a story of a candle.
            But these days, if its flame is set to a fuse,
                  look for the towel-head, right?
                        He's new. He's brown.
                             Must be him.
                          Quick. Send back.

Flory Sandru
Grocery store owner

I run store.
Sell milk, beer, candy, like so.
Take food stamp, yeah.

(Mostrianni)

Sell meat ain't fit for a dog.
Don't matter. Whole store's just window dressing.
He's trading food stamps for cash for meth and cocaine.
A pharmacy he's runnin'. Food's a sideline.
Turned in 7 million in food stamps last year
for 2 million in sales.

(Sirallyi)

I am not going anywhere.
The place I used to live is no longer.
Even the moon and the stars cannot find it.
Bombed. Gone. And the boy who lived there?
The boy whose mother smuggled him out of the country
at 14 to avoid conscription and death,
rolled him in a rug and sent her son away knowing
she would never, ever, ever see him again?
He's gone too.

(Sandru)

Food stamp?
Okay, okay.
Yeah, yeah.
Cash for food stamp.
75 cent f'dolla'.

75 cent, no more.
Cash. Yeah.
Okay, lemme see.
Yeah. Okay.
No problem.

(Mostrianni)

Premium prices are one thing,
it costs extra to operate here.
Extra for the bandits, the insurance.
Extra for the deliveries.
Always extras.
Just keeping my boiler in antacid costs plenty.
So I gotta charge extra, but at least I sell food.

(Sirallyi)

What you see here is a citizen of the US of A.
I have no use for violence.
Does a hawk need wheels?
I have the knowledge, the language to defend myself
against any prejudice this country can cook up
with its perpetual flame.
I am here.

(Sandru)

Meat's bad?
Fruit's bad?
Neighborhood bad.
What you expect?
Take food stamp, yeah.

(Mostrianni)

I'm taking early retirement.
Them Arabs're walking a mine field.
Desert storm's coming, I can feel it.
Drug dealers are real territorial.
You don't piss 'em off,
this here's their happy hunting ground.
I am outta here.
One hairy white ass looks like another after dark.

Fiscal Management

Benjamin Carver
Housing Authority Financial Manager

Like they say in that old commercial, I just do it.
Furnace goes up in smoke, I find the money someplace.
We short on payroll? I find the money.
It's a daily scramble.
Call me Mr. Acronym.
I understand this shit.
CIAP, MROP, HUD, RMC.
Uncle Sam?
Call him Mr. Pockets.
If one pocket turns out empty, it's my job to find another.

Cliff Reins
Partner, Accounting Firm

No, I did *not* sign off on the audit.
Yes, I know, they paid us seven figures.
You ever tried to reassemble coleslaw back into cabbage?

(Carver)

Stress got a cramp on my lower back so bad sometimes
I can't hardly lift the telephone.
10 million, new heating.
3 million, steel doors.
Not handicapped accessible?
12 million. Lead paint? 6 mill more.

                    New steps, one-point-seven.
                    New lights, two-point-four.
               Vandal-proof mailboxes, point-five.
        Government's real generous with grants for what's new,
                but they always be cutting maintenance.
                  So, if stairs start to crumble or
                      railings pop outta the wall,
                 I write a grant for new mailboxes.
                  Borrow from Peter to pay Paul.
                     Nobody really understands,
                     not me, not the auditors.
                   Not the director, not HUD.
                              Nobody.

(Reins)

I put 20 accountants on that matter,
and every time we thought we had a sense of it,
we found another layer in shreds.
Nobody inside is talking,
either they don't know their tails from a pencil sharpener,
or they're too smart to kill the golden goose.
You have what's on the books,
what's known to be off the books,
what's been switched to meet grant goals and switched back,
what's been cooked for the newspapers
and what nobody's ever going to know about.

                                         (Carver)

     It's like strudel all tied up in pretty little red tape packages.
     I move in and out of those accounts like a cockroach at night.
               Takin' a little here, a little there to meet budget,
          pop a few Rolaids and try to anesthetize myself at night

                              with TV and a beer.
                 But nothing can put me to sleep if I know
         it's 10 degrees outside and some mother's window's broke.
                    Tell her the widow budget's busted, too?
                        Leave her babies freezing like that?
                                                   No, sir.

(Reins)

I'm not suggesting indictments,
I think the intentions are in the right place for the most part,
but the financial manager has a high school diploma and a
real nice smile.
Got the job by not asking too many questions.
Man's like a sky light, action's above and below,
he's just in place and a little in need of caulk.
But, no,
I didn't sign.

                                                (Carver)

                                               I just do it
                                        and worry about how
                                       to make it look legal later.
                                        I sleep better that way.

Legalities
___

Mabelle Johnstone
Housing Authority Procurement Clerk

Let me tell you about low cost bidder.
I'm 45-years-old. I grew up in public housing.
My mama was single-female-head-a-household,
eight kids, two bedroom, one bathroom.

Blaine Goodson
Housing Authority Construction Department

Okay, it was illegal, but look it who's living here.
Four, five, six bedroom suites and I'm told to
reside, refloor, rewall, reroof.
Sixteen units.
The whole block's been boarded up for 10 years.
Not a pipe, a furnace or a damn door knob ain't been stolen.
Floors are knee deep in water, plaster and stink.
They gave me six months to turn the block around.
The heat was on me.

(Johnstone)

Eighteen years of us coming up, we got the same toilet seat.
Never got broke or had to change it once.
Now here, once a month it's my job to order toilet seats
for the housing authority.
Maintenance got backorders out the backside, no pun.

(Goodson)

> Lemme ask you -- who do you trust?
> When you got to get on top of something,
> who you want holding the ladder?
> Did I hire my dad to do the job?
> Yeah.
> Nobody cheatin' nobody here.
> I gotta get the job done, I do it.

(Johnstone)

These toilet seats 'bout as strong as your average pizza box,
break the first time anybody sit down.
That's what lowest bidder gets you.

(Goodson)

> We could've *still* been taking bids, but it's done now.
> Look it, who has a house this winter?
> Look how many families we took off the street.
> I'd say, now we got the heat on in the right place.

(Johnstone)

You don't have to be a brain surgeon to
figure out cheaper doesn't always make sense.
Or maybe government think sittin' down to go to the toilet
just one more thing poor folks don't need.

Lessons

Marjorie Gilman
Inner City Teacher

Bent and staggered, the man, like an onion
could bring tears to the eyes,
shedding loose layers of gray stains,
trousers dragging a wake through the dust storm at his feet.
His eyes fixed on another place.
Indigenous to this landscape,
pungent, swaying in the morning stillness.

Larcenia Jacobs
City Services Supervisor

Sister, I got this little clerk,
she so down in the mouth 'cause
her daddy died last summer and her
husband run off. (Poor baby).
She be draggin' her sorry face around here,
not good for nothin' for months.

(Gilman)

"He can't help it," she explains. "He's homeless."
Child to adult, native to foreigner,
she explains to me the day traveler.
I've been schooled to take the long view past his kind.
Only eight-years-old, she takes the short view.
She knows I am out of place.
What kind of place I come from
she doesn't know. She assumes my place is different.
She's is right.

                                            (Jacobs)

               Now I hear she be draggin' her whiney butt
                  off to some psychologist for depression.
                   Ain't <u>that</u> some white woman's luxury.

(Gilman)

These kids come to school knowing how to conjugate
cocksucker,
how to calculate time-served
and knowing about everything there is to know
about how folks
multiply and divide. Kids born knowing too much.
She watches me exit my car and
stamps my passport with a smile.
Together, we climb into the trash can,
metal rattlings all around,
foot-jammed full of yesterday's promises,
wrapped up in the same old news,
a gathering place for roaches and rats,
battleworn, sagging and bruised.
For lack of a better term, we call it school.
                                            (Jacobs)

    She hasn't even begun to learn what I was born knowing.
             My mama worked for $5.00 a day cleaning
                                       white folks' houses,
                         holding white folks' children
       while I'm at home to watch after my brothers and sisters.
                   Everyday her five dollars go like this:
                    35 cent each for the kids for lunches
                                              (that $1.75)
                          $1.50 in the rent envelope.
        The rest pay for supper, clothes and you name it.
              Wasn't no such thing as sick leave or vacation.
                                  No work, no five bucks.

(Gilman)

Funnier still, they call me teacher.

(Jacobs)

My mama never had time off for a sick child,
never for no school program, no cold, no flu.

(Gilman)

Today, I'll teach a little, feed a little.
Try to build a case for why they should learn
what I know.

(Jacobs)

Depression?
What the shit is that.
Baby, this white bitch in need of a reality
lesson real bad.

(Gilman)

It's what I do, like that poor devil on the street.
I can't help it.

Hear It?

Marion Tscarios
Business owner

You can hear it.
Try standing in that park, listen.
When the traffic clears you can hear the sighs.
Listen.
My husband tells me, knock it off, it's the wind.
But I swear, it sighs.
This neighborhood's so tired.

Abdul Shakur Davis
Housing Authority Maintenance

Listen up.
We're comin'.
You look around this neighborhood,
you see only the spot on the ceiling,
what needs fixed.
Well, I see progress grinding like a stone wheel,
grabbing and moaning and starting to roll.

(Tscarios)

Gutters droop from sagging roofs,
exhausted from to many winters.
There's no such thing as bright
and clean is just plain impossible.
The soot from the metal plant, the chemical plant,
and who know what else.
Speckles, dirt all around.
Even the projects, built sturdy brick are boarded up,

graffiti covered. Scarred for life.
I have to remind myself that people live there.
People I know. So sad.

(Davis)

We got the grant for new heating.
No more steam leaks to bring
down the plaster and paint soon as it's up.
That construction gravy train stopped.
We got the new vinyl windows,
no one be stealing for aluminum scrap.
Plastic pipe to replace the copper got took.
We got mailboxes with locks.

(Tscarios)

Freeways passed us by,
then the banks and the insurance agents.
But five minutes from downtown,
we're sitting on pretty cheap land.
Developers tour through like teenagers on the make,
they pretend they're not looking.
We could use a boost but I trust the developers less than the
plants in the flats.
Most of us got a love hate with the filth.
The pollution scares off the yuppies,
preserves our neighborhood.
We could use a few changes,
but we don't want our lives to change.

(Davis)

I grew up here, had none of that.
You dried yourself off with your shirt,
towels were always busy

being stuck in the window leaks, stinkin' of mildew.
I used to lay in bed,
watch the mildew spots on the ceiling grow
till the paint took leave of the wall.

(Tscarios)

Some of the business owners just take their money
home to the suburbs every night when they close up.
Hit and run, I call it. Carpetbaggers.
I live over there, side of that park.
This is my neighborhood that's getting
almost too tired to stand.
Here it?

(Davis)

No more of that, though.
We're comin'.
I can see it.

Poetics

Barbara Barkov
Inner City Teacher

Poetry?
Hello. Knock knock.
You got a screw loose?
These kids can't do poetry.
Most of them can barely read.
Poetry?

> **Falsify Not**
> **Poet**
>
> Each day squeezes
> the sun, bright as a fresh lemon
> dripping with potential,
> a shining tincture
> that sluices through the gloom,
> dissolving stains,
> soothing pain,
> making room
> for hope.

(Barkov)

Look. I know what my job is.
My job is to get these pickaninnies
ready for the test. It's my ass is on the line,
my health care, my retirement. My life and my livelihood.
When the district puts their test scores in the newspaper,
it's my name attached to them.

(Not)

A poet's presence
puts the neighborhood on notice,
taking down dictation
from the babies riding shotgun
on cocked hips,
from elders who liken
memory to present.
From the young who want to
to the wise who have.
Poetry is observation,
noting
what is shared,
what's shrunk or swollen,
itemizing matters given,
stocked, and stolen.
The poet stops to look and listen
to the fringes,
the extremes,
and all the in-betweens.

(Barkov)

Thanks to Bill Gates' billions
my salary is tied like a limp cat
to a stone sinking in a river of mess.
I don't have time for any of your poetry nonsense.
Or science, for that matter.
Math and reading.
That's what they test and what I teach.
3 hours of each.
No recess.
No scissors. No markers.
Nothing that can be used as a weapon.

(Not)

> Drawing taut
> the slender threads of truth,
> with rhymes and reason,
> speaking for and to,
> weaving tender bridges.
> Understanding.

(Barkov)

Poetry? Good luck with that.
Poetry may work for some kids.
But, reality check!
Not these kids.
Get a clue.

> **(Not)**
>
> Poetry is real.

Where's It All Going?

The Bishop
Preacher

Those projects' too strong for the wrecker's ball,
too stubborn to fall down.
So much violence comes out of these buildings.
Circle out and come back in.
Nowhere else to go.
Everyday's a fight,
somewheres.
In or between these buildings.
Poof.
A match on a drop of gin,
flash,
and it's over,
but for a kite string of smoke.
Our buildings,
our young men.
Where's it all goin'?
Around and around.

Ryan Wheeler
Age 10

Here's my snowman poem.

My snowman can't read.
My snowman can't walk.
My snowman can't sing.
My snowman can't talk.

My snowman stands still,
and he can melt.
He wears a baseball hat
and a Santa belt.

Ramiro Martinez
Resident, Age 10

Here's my snowman poem.

My snowman can't dance he points
his gun, make all the blood and robbers
run and the snow get red and he say
you better off dead!!!

He not rude he's a dude.
He can melt and he can't feel when he
get hit with a belt he knows a stripper
she works the Big Dipper
He cold as snow what do he know
he can't eat pizza.

CPSIA information can be obtained at www.ICGtesting.com
Printed in the USA
LVOW10s0003240715

447468LV00004B/85/P